Cello Time Christmas

a stockingful of 32 easy pieces for cello

Kathy and David Blackwell

illustrations by Alan Rowe

Welcome to **Cello Time Christmas**. You'll find:

- 32 well-known Christmas carols and pieces with words to sing along
- solos and duets using finger patterns 0–1–34 and 0–12–4
- easy chord symbols for guitar or keyboard accompaniment; these chords are not compatible with the CD performances
- a CD with performances to listen or play along to; the varied accompaniments use piano, guitar, drums, and bass
- piano accompaniments available in a separate volume

Using the CD:

- all carols and pieces are played through twice, except those pieces which include a **D.C.** or **D.S. al Fine**, and 'Hogmanay Reel', which are performed once only
- each carol and piece has a short introduction and a link between the verses
- where there are duet parts, these are mostly added in the second verse
- Tuning track: track 33.

Performers: cello Tom Morter; guitar Pete Vecchietti; double bass/bass guitar Mike Chilcott; percussion/drumkit Jon Buxton; piano David Blackwell. Grateful thanks to Pete Vecchietti for devising the CD arrangements of Nos. 9, 26, 27, and 29.

MUSIC DEPARTMENT

OXFORD
UNIVERSITY PRESS

OXFORD
UNIVERSITY PRESS

Great Clarendon Street, Oxford OX2 6DP, England

Oxford University Press is a department of the University of Oxford.
It furthers the University's aim of excellence in research, scholarship,
and education by publishing worldwide

Oxford is a registered trade mark of Oxford University Press
in the UK and in certain other countries

16

ISBN 978–0–19–336932–0

Music and text origination by
Barnes Music Engraving Ltd, East Sussex
Printed in Great Britain on acid-free paper by
Halstan & Co. Ltd, Amersham, Bucks.

Contents

Piece/ track no.		Page no.
1	Hark! the herald-angels sing	4
2	The holly and the ivy (*duet*)	5
3	Ding dong! merrily on high	6
4	Andrew mine, Jasper mine	6
5	Silent night (*duet*)	7
6	I saw three ships (*duet*)	8
7	O little town of Bethlehem	8
8	Once in royal David's city	9
9	Go tell it on the mountain	9
10	We wish you a merry Christmas	10
11	Shepherds watched	10
12	O Christmas tree (*duet*)	11
13	We three kings	12
14	Bethl'em lay a-sleeping (*duet*)	13
15	Good King Wenceslas	13
16	Infant holy, infant lowly (*duet*)	14
17	Deck the hall	14
18	O come, all ye faithful (*duet*)	15
19	Away in a manger (*duet*)	16
20	The first Nowell	16
21	Zither Carol	17
22	God rest you merry, gentlemen	17
23	Skaters' Waltz (*duet*)	18
24	Dance of the Reed Pipes	19
25	While shepherds watched their flocks	20
26	Children, go! (*duet*)	20
27	Child in a manger (*duet*)	21
28	Jingle, bells	22
29	Mary had a baby	22
30	Christmas Calypso (*duet*)	23
31	Hogmanay Reel	24
32	Auld Lang Syne	24
33	Tuning track (A—D—G—C)	

1. Hark! the herald-angels sing

Felix Mendelssohn (1809–47)

Hark! the he - rald - an - gels sing __ Glo - ry to the new-born King; Peace on earth and

mer - cy mild, __ God and sin - ners re - con - ciled: Joy - ful all ye na - tions rise, __

Join the tri - umph of the skies, With th'an-gel - ic host pro-claim, Christ is __ born in

Beth - le - hem. Hark! the he - rald - an - gels sing Glo - ry __ to the new-born King.

2. The holly and the ivy

English trad.

3. Ding dong! merrily on high

16th-century French melody

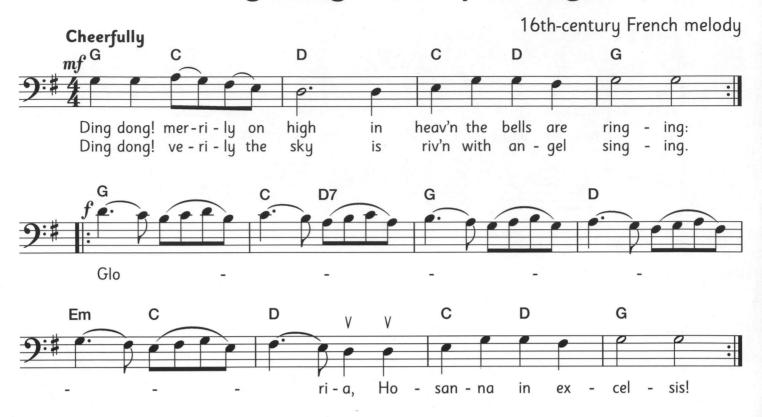

4. Andrew mine, Jasper mine

Moravian carol

Andrew mine, Jasper mine: words by C. K. Offer from *Three Moravian Carols*
© Oxford University Press 1962. Reproduced by permission of Oxford University Press.

5. Silent night

Franz Gruber (1787–1863)

Si - lent night, ho - ly night, All is calm,

all is bright; Round yon vir - gin moth - er and child.

Ho - ly in - fant so ten - der and mild, Sleep in

hea - ven - ly peace,___ Sleep___ in hea - ven - ly peace.

6. I saw three ships

English trad.

Like a dance

I saw three ships come sail-ing in On Christ-mas Day, on Christ-mas Day, I saw three ships come sail-ing in On Christ-mas Day in the morn-ing.

7. O little town of Bethlehem

English trad.

Gently

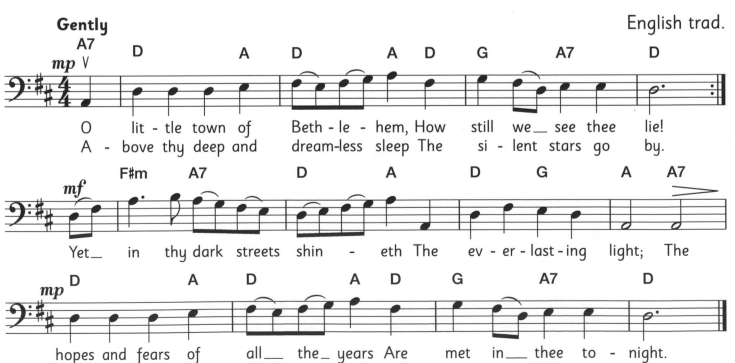

O lit-tle town of Beth-le-hem, How still we_ see thee lie!
A-bove thy deep and dream-less sleep The si-lent stars go by.

Yet_ in thy dark streets shin - eth The ev-er-last-ing light; The

hopes and fears of all_ the_ years Are met in_ thee to - night.

8. Once in royal David's city

H. J. Gauntlett (1805–76)

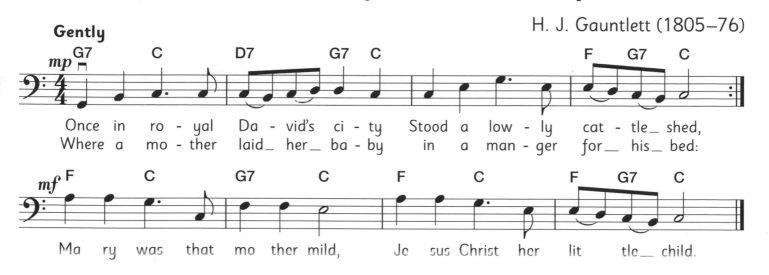

Once in ro - yal Da - vid's ci - ty Stood a low - ly cat - tle_ shed,
Where a mo - ther laid_ her_ ba - by in a man - ger for_ his_ bed:

Ma - ry was that mo - ther mild, Je - sus Christ her lit - tle_ child.

9. Go tell it on the mountain

American trad.

Go tell it on the moun - tain, o - ver the hills and ev - 'ry - where;

Go tell it on the moun - tain that Je - sus Christ is born!

Shep-herds kept their watch - ing o'er wand-'ring flocks by night; Be -

- hold from out of hea - ven there shone a ho - ly light:____

10. We wish you a merry Christmas

11. Shepherds watched

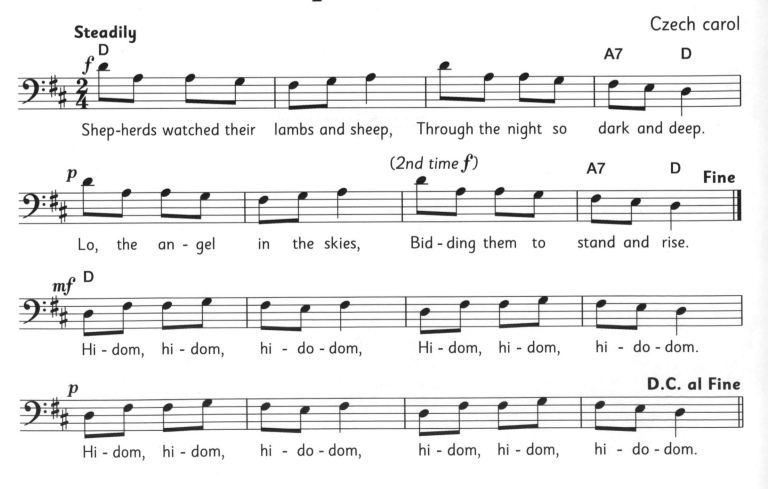

12. O Christmas tree

German trad.

O Christ-mas tree, O Christ-mas tree, With faith-ful leaves un – chan-ging!

Not on-ly green in sum-mer's heat But in the win – ter's snow and sleet: O

Christ-mas tree, O Christ-mas tree, With faith-ful leaves un – chan-ging!

13. We three kings

Stately

J. H. Hopkins (1820–91)

We three kings of O - ri - ent are; Bear - ing gifts we tra - verse a - far Field and foun - tain, moor and moun - tain, Fol - low - ing yon - der star: O_____ star of won - der, star of night, Star with roy - al beau - ty bright, West - ward lead - ing, still pro - ceed - ing, Guide us to thy per - fect light.

14. Bethl'em lay a-sleeping

Polish carol

Simply

mp arco

pizz.

mp

Beth-l'em lay a-sleep-ing,

long, so long a-go, | Twink-ling stars were peep-ing, | long, so long a-go,

When to earth a ba-by came the | lit-tle Je-sus was his name, So | long, long a-go.

15. Good King Wenceslas

Piae Cantiones (1582)

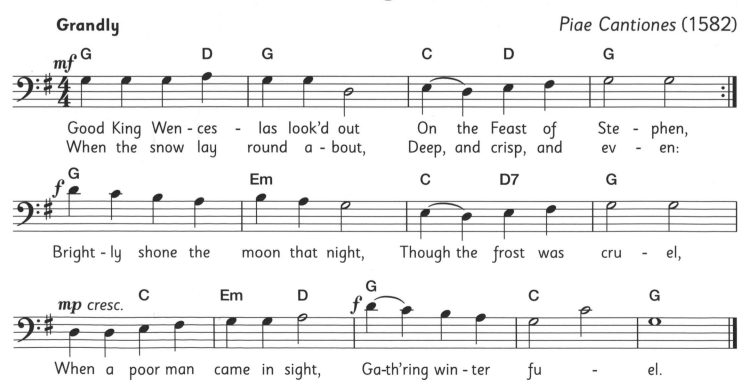

Grandly

mf G   D   G   C   D   G

Good King Wen-ces-las look'd out   On the Feast of Ste-phen,
When the snow lay round a-bout,   Deep, and crisp, and ev-en:

f G   Em   C   D7   G

Bright-ly shone the moon that night,   Though the frost was cru-el,

mp cresc. C   Em   D   *f* G   C   G

When a poor man came in sight,   Ga-th'ring win-ter fu-el.

16. Infant holy, infant lowly

Polish carol

17. Deck the hall

Welsh trad.

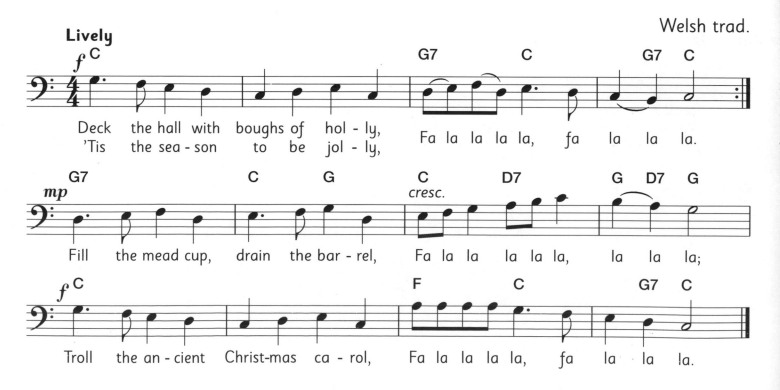

18. O come, all ye faithful

J. F. Wade (c.1711–86)

Joyfully

O come, all ye faith-ful, Joy-ful and tri-um-phant, O come ye, O come ye to Beth-le-hem; Come and be-hold him Born the King of An-gels: O come, let us a-dore him, O come, let us a-dore him, O come let us a-dore him, Christ the Lord!

19. Away in a manger

William J. Kirkpatrick (1838–1921)

20. The first Nowell

English trad.

21. Zither Carol

Czech carol

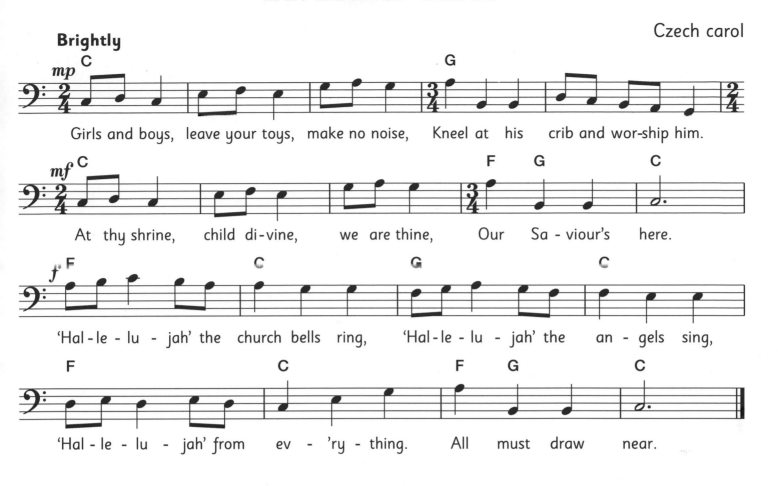

Girls and boys, leave your toys, make no noise, Kneel at his crib and wor-ship him.

At thy shrine, child di-vine, we are thine, Our Sa-viour's here.

'Hal-le-lu-jah' the church bells ring, 'Hal-le-lu-jah' the an-gels sing,

'Hal-le-lu-jah' from ev-'ry-thing. All must draw near.

22. God rest you merry, gentlemen

English trad.

God rest you mer-ry, gen-tle-men, Let no-thing you dis-may, For

Je-sus Christ our Sa-viour Was born up-on this day, To save us all from

Sa-tan's power When we were gone a-stray: O___ ti-dings of com-fort and

joy, com-fort and joy, O___ ti-dings of com-fort and joy.

23. Skaters' Waltz

Emil Waldteufel (1837–1915)

24. Dance of the Reed Pipes

(from the *Nutcracker* ballet)

Pyotr Ilyich Tchaikovsky (1840–93)

25. While shepherds watched their flocks

Lively

Este's Psalter (1592)

While shep-herds watched their flocks by night, All seat-ed on the ground, The
an - gel of the Lord came down, And glo-ry shone a - round.

26. Children, go!

Spiritual

Lively

Child - ren, go where I send thee! How shall I

send thee? I'm gon-na send thee one by one, one for the lit-tle bit-ty

ba - by boy, Born, born,_ born in Beth-le - hem.

27. Child in a manger

Celtic trad.

Child in a man - ger, Je - sus our Sa - viour,

Born of a vir - gin ho - ly and mild;

Sent from the high - est, Come down in glo - ry;

Tell the glad sto - ry, Wel-come the child.

28. Jingle, bells

J. Pierpont (1822–93)

Happily

Jin-gle, bells, jin-gle, bells, jin-gle all the way; Oh, what fun it

is to ride in a one-horse o-pen sleigh!__ Jin-gle, bells, jin-gle, bells,

jin-gle all the way; Oh, what fun it is to ride in a one-horse o-pen sleigh!

29. Mary had a baby

American trad.

Lively

Ma-ry had a ba-by, Yes, Lord! Ma-ry had a ba-by, Yes, my Lord!

Ma-ry had a ba-by, Yes, Lord! Peo-ple keep a-com-in', and the train done gone!

30. Christmas Calypso

Kathy & David Blackwell

So dance the Christ-mas Ca-lyp-so in the sun,__ Je-sus is born for ev-'ry-one;__ Sing out with joy and stamp your feet,__ move to the ca-lyp-so beat!_ Way back in Beth-le-hem, in a sim-ple sta-ble, Je-sus, that ba-by boy,_ came to save us all! So dance the

Fine

D.%. al Fine

31. Hogmanay Reel

Kathy & David Blackwell

32. Auld Lang Syne

Scottish trad.

Should auld ac-quain-tance be for-got, and nev - er brought to mind? Should

auld ac-quain-tance be for-got, for the sake of auld lang syne? For

auld____ lang____ syne, my dear, for auld____ lang____ syne; We'll

tak' a cup o' kind - ness yet, for the sake of auld lang syne.